Play a Song for Me

Mike Gould

Folens

Editor: Kay Macmullan
Layout artist: Suzanne Ward
Cover design: John Hawkins
Illustrations: Josephine Blake

First published 2004 by Folens Limited.

British Library Cataloguing in Publication Data. A catalogue record for this publication is available from the British Library.

ISBN 1 84303 694–0

Contents

The story so far

If you haven't read an *On the edge* book before:
The stories take place in and around a row of shops and
buildings called Pier Parade in Brightsea, right next to the
sea. There's Big Fry, the fish and chip shop; Drop Zone, the
drop-in centre for local teenagers; Macmillan's, the sweet
and souvenir shop; Anglers' Haven, the fishing tackle
shop; the Surf 'n' Skate shop and, of course, the Brightsea
Beach Bar.

If you have read an *On the edge* book you may have met
some of these people before.

Zelda: *likes dark clothes and might be considered a goth by
some, but she prefers to think of herself as original.
Zelda goes to Alexandra Community College.*

Ryan: *a young singer, trying to make a living on the seafront
at Brightsea, and in the shopping centre.*

So, what's been going on?
Zelda doesn't mix that well with some of the people at
school; the in-crowd think she's too weird to hang out
with, but she doesn't care and she doesn't need them.

What happens in this story?
Zelda is on the seafront enjoying Ryan's singing and
guitar-playing when a couple of teenagers turn up,
determined to put a stop to Ryan's playing. But when one
of them tries to smash Ryan's guitar, Zelda can't stand by
and watch…

1

Music man

Zelda walked away from the shops.

She was going down to the seafront.

She wanted to get some fresh air before

she went home.

She could hear music.

What was it?

A guitar?

She carried on walking.

The music sounded good.

And someone was singing.

On the seafront Zelda saw the

person singing.

It was a young man.

He was playing a guitar.

He was really good!

His hands moved very fast.

His voice was good too.

When he ended his song,

Zelda clapped.

The young man looked at Zelda and

said, "Thank you."

Zelda looked around her.

She was the only one listening!

It was a young man. He was playing a guitar.

Zelda said, "Can you play a song
for me?"

"OK," the young man said.

He began the song.

It was quite slow but it had a
happy tune.

Just then, a boy and a girl came up.

They looked about the same age
as Zelda.

The boy was quite tall.

He started laughing.

"That's rubbish, mate!" he shouted.

That's rubbish, mate!

Zelda didn't say anything at first.

She thought to herself, "Is he joking?"

Then the boy spoke again.

"Why don't you shut up? You'll scare the seagulls!"

He laughed loudly at his joke.

But the young man with the guitar didn't stop.

He carried on playing.

That's when the trouble began.

2

Troublemaker

The tall boy looked cross.

He spoke to the young man with

the guitar.

"This is our beach. You're a stranger.

Stop playing and go away!"

The girl didn't say anything.

She looked a bit ashamed.

The tall boy stepped forward.

There were some coins in a hat on
the ground.

It was money that people had given to
the young man.

The tall boy picked up the hat.

The young man stopped playing.

"That's my money!" he said.

"It's mine now!" said the tall boy.

"Give it back," said the girl.

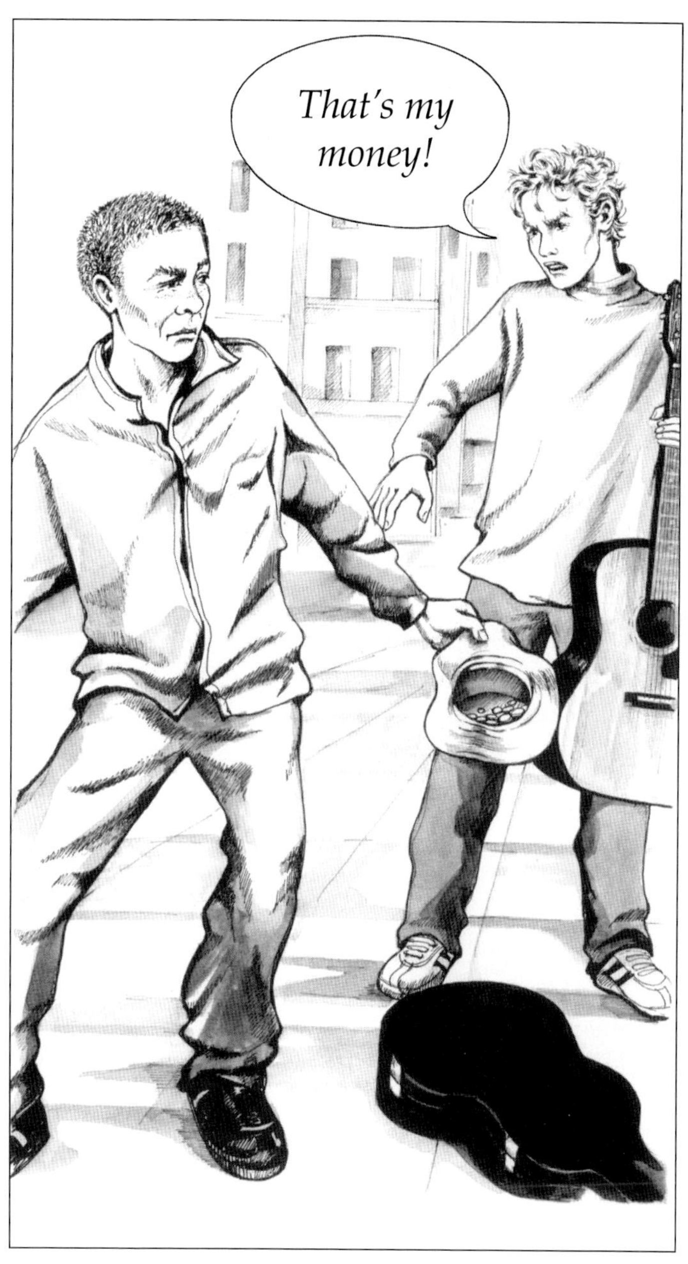

That's my money!

"OK," said the tall boy.

Then, he turned the hat upside down.

All the coins fell out of the hat.

They rolled everywhere.

"Ha ha!" laughed the tall boy.

The young man put his guitar down.

Then he started to try to pick up

the coins.

Zelda helped him.

All the coins fell out of the hat.

Then Zelda noticed the tall boy.

He was standing by the guitar.

He raised his foot.

"Watch this!" he said to the girl.

"Watch me smash this guitar!"

Zelda stood up.

She thought, "This isn't fair."

She had to do something.

She had to do something quickly.

3

Hard case

Zelda picked up the guitar case.

The case was heavy.

The tall boy still had his foot over

the guitar.

He wasn't looking at Zelda.

He was too busy laughing.

Zelda moved close to him.

Then she swung the case.

She swung it hard and fast.

The case hit the tall boy.

"Ow!" he cried.

He stepped back.

"That hurt!" he said.

Zelda put the case down.

"You deserved it!"

The tall boy looked really mad.

Really cross.

"I'll get you for that!" he said to Zelda.

He started to walk towards her.

Ow!
You deserved it!

Zelda picked up the case again.

"Go on then!" she said. "Go on. Try to get me if you want. I don't mind. I will hit you again."

The tall boy stopped.

He didn't know what to do.

Zelda looked really cross too.

"Just watch it!" the tall boy said.

"Come on," said the girl. "Let's go."

Come on.
Let's go.

The tall boy looked at Zelda for
a moment.

"It didn't hurt anyway," he said.

But he still wasn't standing up straight.

The tall boy and the girl walked away.

Zelda put down the guitar case.

It was heavy!

The young man looked at her.

"Thanks!" he said.

4

Coffee break

Zelda and the young man sat in the 3Bs bar.

"You saved my life!" said the young man.

"Not really," said Zelda.

"Well, you saved my guitar. My guitar is my life!"

"No problem," said Zelda. "It wasn't fair of that boy."

"What's your name?" asked the young man.

"Zelda," said Zelda.

"That's a strange name," said the young man.

"I'm a strange person!" said Zelda.

They both laughed.

"What's your name?" asked Zelda.

"Ryan," said the young man.

"Pleased to meet you," said Zelda.

And they shook hands.

What's your name?
Ryan.

Then Zelda saw something.

There was a note stuck to the window.

It read:

"You could play here!" said Zelda.

"I'm not good enough," said Ryan.

"Yes, you are," said Zelda. "Don't

listen to what that stupid boy said."

You could play
here!

Ryan looked unsure.

"There he is," said Zelda.

"Who?" asked Ryan.

"The manager. Mel."

Zelda pointed to a man behind the bar.

"Go on!" she said.

Ryan didn't move.

"Go on," she said again. "Now is your chance!"

5

Your song

That night, Ryan played and sang at the bar.

Zelda watched him.

All the people in the bar clapped and cheered.

Ryan looked pleased.

"Can you play here next week?" asked Mel.

Mel was the owner of the bar.

"Yes, if you want me to," said Ryan.

"Of course I do. Everyone thinks

you're great," said Mel.

The people in the bar clapped and

cheered again.

"Can I play one last song?"

asked Ryan.

"Yes," said Mel. "Go on."

Zelda waited for the song.

She wondered, "What will he play?"

Ryan spoke to the people who were in

the bar.

"This song is for Zelda, " he said.

This song is
for Zelda.

He pointed at Zelda.

"It's called, 'You've Got a Friend'."

Zelda blushed.

Ryan began to sing.

But then Zelda saw someone.

It was the girl from earlier.

She was watching from the back of the

bar near the door.

Zelda thought, "Will that girl do

something bad?"

Ryan was still playing.

Will that girl do something bad?

But Zelda kept her eyes on the girl.

The girl just stared at Ryan.

Then the song ended.

Ryan smiled.

The people in the bar cheered

and clapped.

"More! More!" they called.

Zelda looked at the girl.

The girl raised her hands.

Slowly, the girl started to clap.

She clapped louder and louder.

Then, she looked at Zelda and smiled.

The tall boy was nowhere to be seen.

Glossary

(to) blush	(to) go red in the face
(to) get (someone)	(to) attack or get revenge
hard case	someone who is tough
rubbish	no good
watch it	be careful or I'll do something to you